Meaningful Sounds
New and Collected Poems

Nathan Polsky

Volume I

Copyright © 2013 by Nathan Polsky
All rights reserved. No part of this book may be reproduced, scanned, or distributed in any printed or electronic form without permission.
First Edition: May 2013
Published by Suncoast Digital Press, Inc., Sarasota, Florida
Printed in the United States of America
ISBN: 978-1-939237-17-0

Cover Art
"Purple & Yellow Color Blocks" by Debbie Dannheisser
Fine Art Gallery, www.debbiedannheisser.com

To Janet

Foreword

It's common, we know from experience, to describe and picture advanced age with small words and images of endings.

This can be true through the eyes and insight of the custodian of that age. This can also be true through the eyes and assumptions seeing and experiencing another of significant age.

Nathan Polsky, the Poet, writes his words and paints his word images on the truly large canvas of life. He tells his truths, expresses his regrets, cites his appreciations, and embraces his ambitions with a clarity and gusto to which we might all aspire at any age.

> Misty dark shields our moonlight's cry
> for peace and kiss of kindness's
> soft and feathery touch.

Stand back from his work and take the large perspective of it. Stand up close and see the details that represent the energies of his long life. Stand at midrange and imagine capturing yourself and your life with such verve when the time comes. In doing so, enjoy the shared truths he brings to his brave accomplishment.

To read Mr. Polsky's poetry is to know the man and his life. To see what he sees is for all of us both an adventure and an opportunity for insight, learning, and the joy of art.

George H. Schofield, Ph.D.
Human & Organizational Development
Author, *After 50 It's Up To Us,* © 2007

Meet the Author

Nathan Polsky shares his thoughts about how this collection came about, and reads one of his poems.
Visit - http://youtu.be/KkpOT8bd70Y

Preface

It's such a joy to be wrapped
in a blanket of private silence,
so solitude can water emerging seeds
of a poem.

It's a thrill to cup creative hands together
and mold a patty of memory, experience,
observation, thoughts, insights and reflection
… even fantasy and comedy…
with a stanza or more
of something worth sharing,
from the light-hearted
to the serious.

Nathan Polsky

Contents

Foreword V
Preface VII
Independent 1
Simple Truth 2
End Game 3
Backwards, March! 4
Destiny 6
A Love Story 8
The Brink 10
Journey 11
Now Where Was I? 12
Scenario 13
Silent Friends 14
Unfair Fight 16
Regret 18
Dream 19
Outrageously Strange 20
Lighten Up 21
Re-Lived 22
Wishful Thinking 25
A Young Man's Song 26
Soft Sell 28
Walking Books 29
Favoritism 30
Hello, It's Me 32
A Bombardier's Story 34
I Give Up! 36
Rambling 38
Still More Rambling 39
Shy Companion 40
Keep It Clean 41
Solution 42

CHOICES	43
RETRIEVAL	44
VOID	45
MIA AND DVD	46
AWAITED NEWS	48
EXIT	49
OUR WINTER'S TALE	50
CITY SONG	52
BOOK LEARNING	53
PUPPY LOVE	54
BALM	55
AND I APPROVE THIS MESSAGE!	56
MUSING	58
APPLAUSE	59
INFLATED FUN	60
PRIMITIVE ART	61
HOW DO I LOVE ME? (A BRAGGART'S VOICE)	62
FLOW	64
LAUGH	66
CONTINUITY	67
RESPECT	68
A SHORT BIOGRAPHY	70
ONE AND ONLY	72
NEW YEAR'S GRACIOUS COMPANY	73
BUILDING BLOCKS	74
AND SO IT IS WRITTEN	75
REMEMBERED	76
SEASONS	77
FORTUNE'S TWIST	78
FUNNY	80
VISTA	81
SOME NERVE!	82

Wishes	84
Expression	85
Forgotten	86
Preference	87
I Thought You'd Want To Know	88
Homage	89
Metaphorically Speaking	90
Poet's Aid	92
Re-Wind	93
Meaningful Sounds	94
Last Grad Standing	95
Blueprint	96
Wheel Of Fortune	97
Social Animal	98
Transported	99
More Than Just Friends	100
Withdrawal	101
Passing Encounter	102
Merry You Know What	103
Judgments	104
Home Sweet Home	106
Prove It!	107
Floral Journey	108
Not A Bad Fad	109
Hm-m-m, Now Let Me See...	110
Enigma	111
Image And Truth	112
Awesome	113
Hello Again	114
Poetic Expression	115
Alternatives	116
Share	117
About The Author	119

Independent

While passing by a leafy bush
I noticed something strange:
a maverick leaf above the rest
impatient for a change.

It seemed so restless, waving so
and catching every breeze;
it showed a spirit with its own mind,
looking down as if to tease.

If leaves could speak and share their thoughts
what would they think and say,
about this dancer proud and tall
and its independent way ?

I felt delight, but pitied, too,
for despite its rooted fate,
it yearned for freedom and playful will,
and I envied such a trait!

So, marveling as I watched in awe,
a witness to this show,
it seemed as if it noticed me
and wished to say "Hello!".

Simple Truth

From here to there the daisies cry
beneath a storm's obsessive mirth,
with hapless fears and helpless sway,
the peace awash in sun ray's dearth.

The petals fret in puzzled awe
at Mother's inundating play,
and frown their frowns impatiently
for warmth that means another day.

But a lesson's here for those who see,
that Nature's plan is stern and clear:
The rain and sun and earth itself
each helps provide us smile and tear.

End Game

I've done my best, I've run my race,
there's more time behind than fore.
I'm done with working and worried days,
and being shown the door.

The many years seeking soothing peace,
the match of self and place;
the growing pains to escape the traps,
while showing a placid face.

It's what most of us must daily do,
intent to make a life
with pride intact and plodding on,
despite the stress and strife.

It was a crazy game of chance,
combined with nerve and sweat.
I wouldn't want to repeat the trip:
I've fully paid my debt.

My patient wife was by my side
and shared the darks and lights
without complaints and hope intact.
We shared the sleepless nights.

So, my perspective makes it clear:
persistence wins the game.
I'm happy now with poems and art,
tho' the world forgets my name.

Backwards, March!

Hello, I must be going now
Goodbye I'll stay awhile.
Why don't you sit and also stand.
An inch is still a mile.

Your friend is foe, the desert's wet,
so smile and cry for me
Your wager's down, you lost your bet!
My lock still has no key.

The daylight's dim, the night's aglow.
Drink in the view a bit.
The insider's out, the high is low:
A miss is still a hit.

My hunger yearns for less, you see;
my shoes fit like a glove.
Hello, hello, I cannot stay:
I hate and still I love.

What's up is down, what's here is there:
it's hard and soft at once.
You are not mine, but yours to keep:
I am just a hatted dunce.

My older years are young and firm;
my hunger yearns for less.
Hello, hello, I cannot stay!
I curse but yet I bless.

I dance on embers hot yet cold:
I cannot keep from crying.
The sad is real, the laugh rings false.
I sell but you're not buying.

My shadow's long, the moon's behind;
the trick was in the knowing.
Better late the early bird.
Hello, I must be going.

Destiny

The roses given, the cheers so loud,
how thrilling it would be;
adoring crowds, my name to sign,
and my folks so proud of me.

The homers hit and arias sung;
the masterpiece I did.
My symphonic piece so softly played
(I'm called "that genius kid").

My touchdown won the game we played
(I kicked the ball to score).
I swam so fast to win the gold,
I still hear the shouts and roar.

I jockeyed well and won the race,
my horse just knew my skill.
That silver cup and scarf of rose,
just proved I'm master still.

I win my fights and knock them out
(there's no one else to beat).
My holes in one are talked of still:
the books record this feat!

The sums I've won with cards and dice
cause legendary awe.
No player dares to play with me:
One game, and they're out the door!

I jump so high to score my points
(that hoop is a friend with me).
I twist and turn and make my shots,
the scoreboard's great to see!

The plans I draw for malls and bridge
bring tons of smiles and praise.
They offered me a special prize!
I'll cherish all my days.

That Russian champ of chess dared me
to back my claim of skill.
He'd show me how that game was played.
(I think he's shaking still!)

The novels, poems and songs I've done
are taught to all today.
My plays and films add lustre still
(I'm humble yet, they say!).

Nation's leaders come to talk
and ask for my advice.
I freely point to errors made.
(Their thanks, I think, are nice!)

I've been the first to stand on Mars
(my training paid off big!).
When I return, I let others go:
I didn't want to be a pig.

As I thought of underwater stunts,
I heard a voice so cool.
It was my wife just there to say
"Wake up, you damn old fool!".

A Love Story

I remember well her auburn hair,
her upturned nose, as well;
her arching back, her greenish eyes…
(My God, there's much to tell!)

A lonely boy, I looked at her
and saw the hopeless gap.
I never dreamed we'd ever fall
in Fate's ensnaring trap.

Our lives, however, touched at times.
Our paths began to merge.
We felt a comfort and an ease.
I felt my passion surge.

We saw and shared this friendly bond,
as months just frittered by.
But we each had many things to do.
(Hindsight makes me sigh.)

As time went by a drift began.
A story that's not new.
The army, school and this and that
was shielding each from view.

So years flew by and we went our ways
pursuing our own fates.
There still was not a tiny hint
that we could end up mates.

We each had others in our lives
(A fact we cannot hide);
but none of them seemed right for us.
Our dreams were pushed aside.

Then puppets that we seemed to be,
once more by chance we met
and there she was alive and cute,
our story not finished yet.

We returned once more to where we were,
before our split began;
turned back the clock and loved anew:
I was a happy man.

We married and began our life
as only buddies can.
I write these words to celebrate
our sixty-third year span.

The Brink

Will doom times come and imperiled earth
approaches its glory's end,
a victim of its plundering dumb
and selfish selves to tend?

This gift of home, so right for us,
this miracle orbiting speck,
may perish by our hands alone
if ignoring wisdom's beck.

There's so much cause for unease and fear,
so many ways to see
the logic of the fruits of greed,
for which we pay a fee.

Nature's prize of flesh and brain
to flout, I think, is odd,
like killing others unlike us
or with competing views of "God".

The "brotherhood" we speak and seek
is but a hopeless dream.
We've tried and sought, since we began;
it's useless, it would seem.

So, if not destroyed by nature's rage,
or other man-made cause,
I do confess with sadness real,
our future gives me pause.

There's little time to make amends,
our skills for death are real.
If sanity and wisdom go awry,
there'll be no bells to peal!

Journey

On journey's road that's traveled on
by each and every one;
the forks we take and turns we make
we choose since we've begun.

We drive our lives with hope and wish,
we note the signs and lights;
and along the way perhaps we stop
to gaze at all the sights.

But many times there are no hints
to tell us where we are;
our paths are vague and guess we must
driving our little car.

Crossroads and streets are there to see,
but still we try to guess:
it's luck and chance that steer our wheel:
it's confusing, I confess.

Life's choices, thus, this puzzle makes;
sometimes we can't control.
We drive yet we are driven, too,
and take a back seat role.

We make wrong turns and back-track, too,
there are no maps to use.
We sometimes stop to ask for help,
but almost all refuse.

So where we finally come to rest
results from hit or miss:
a left turn here, a right one there,
we owe our fate a kiss!

Now Where Was I?

My energy level has gone to the devil,
I can't help it if I'm such a grouch.
I feel so tired and sleepy
it's hard to keepy
from napping on floor or on couch.

I need pills or excitement
or some kind of enticement
before I can be my old self.
I watch these kids swinging
and hear those jerks singing
and just feel like I've been put on the shelf.

Scenario

In a nutshell, it's easy does it:
for growing pains is now frozen in time.
The wetness behind ears is the opening salvo.
and, at the least, a fanning out as memory
records and takes notes.

The pecking order forms, and life is on probation
and up for grabs,
as unfolding fortune looks askance
at the receipt of its welcome-wagon gifts.

Starting from scratch at a learning saunter,
then, a brisker walk as life's hand beckons.
enticing with purrs and yielding walls,
with failure and loss in hot pursuit.

Innocent's fond farewell forebodes
the surer-footed and carefree,
or the hard scrabble bashing by destiny's
bullying spite.

Silent Friends

What would life be like without such things
that we take for granted now:
the little things, the useful things,
that serve without a bow!

We don't think twice when needs arise:
we know what's there to use.
They're there in drawer and box and bin:
our friends like hook and fuse.

They're on the desk or near at hand,
all well within our reach.
They do their job without complaint
(I do not mean to preach!).

When problems come, as come they will,
these tools do serve us well.
Whatever did we do before:
I really cannot tell.

There'll always be inventive minds,
which see a need to fill;
we owe them much, there' s more to come,
for time does not stand still.

Spray cans are very handy things,
cling wrap and aluminum foil;
the battery, too, must not be missed,
or anti-squeaky oil.

Scissors, pads and dry-erase,
cork screw and steel wool pad;
veggie peeler, suction cup,
pill-splitter's not a fad.

Can opener, matchsticks and the bulb,
garlic presses, too;
remote control, the fax machine,
the Band-Aid was a coup.

The stapler, glue stick, rubber band,
the plastic box and bag;
felt-tip marker, two-side tape,
coffee maker's jag.

The ball-point pen and paper clip,
the tea bag and credit card;
correction fluid, Post-it notes,
each makes our lives less hard.

Clippers are for cutting nails,
ear plugs to curb the racket:
the calculator is a joy,
and the single-portion packet.

Nutcracker, shoe horn, toilet plunger,
nail file and measuring spoon.
Let's not forget the cell phone, too,
for photos, talk and tune.

Eraser, sponge and paper towel
and that ever-handy flashlight;
pliers, hammer, screw drivers,
and then there is the nite-lite.

So, there's my list to brag about,
we use them well with ease,
these common friends who serve us well
and make our lives a breeze!

These things are but a small review;
I skimmed what came to mind.
You can add your own to these:
I know there's more to find.

Unfair Fight

A memorable test of wits and guile,
that shattered and humbled me,
was when I tried to outsmart a raccoon,
and it said, "Oh yeah! Let's see!".

My garbage and trash were stored outside
beneath a wooden lid.
The raccoon laughed at naive me
and said, "Oh, you innocent kid!".

I could hear the laugh in my puzzled mind,
and thought I'd try again.
This time I'd place a heavy weight.
How could he master men?

Sure enough, the surprise next day
was garbage on the ground.
The little twerp just helped itself
without a single sound!

It was now a challenging game of smarts:
a grown man against a critter.
My pride was now in full alert
to see who was mentally fitter.

Next, I pushed a stick in the latch
so the cover was locked fast and firm.
I would have liked to see its face that night,
when there was no place to squirm.

But the daylight told me my trick had failed:
the pest just removed the wedge,
and again just thumbed his runny nose
and pushed me over the edge.

Finally, in a shattered state,
I decided to end this bout.
I gave the little devil its due
and I didn't put any garbage out!

Regret

I wish I could undo the past
and get a second chance.
I worked so hard to get ahead
as if I were in a trance!

I did not stint with efforts spent
at projects self -assigned:
those hours stolen from the day
that made a demon mind.

The price I paid to find my way
was a penalty I now well know.
I lost the nectar and the joy
of watching a family grow!

I wish I was there as husband and dad,
far more than time allowed.
I missed my two girls' growing years,
for which I am not proud.

My wife was patient as a saint,
she gave her best to all;
with wisdom, patience and guts as well,
she oversaw rise and fall.

So now I sit and scan the past
and wish for a second chance.
Life's regrets make me so very sad
for I missed our song and dance.

Dream

Misty dark shields our moonlight's cry
for peace and kiss of kindness's
soft and feathery touch.

Outrageously Strange

Out of a wall, a foot protrudes,
some balls of cotton hang low;
a mound of pebbles are scattered around,
whose meanings we're supposed to know.

The crumpled sheets above iron grills,
a mannequin's head stares back;
empty coffee cans are stacked
on top of a box that's black.

A stuffed goat is in a tire encased,
a shark is frozen in plastic;
a skull is encrusted with diamonds' glint
(the artist thought that was fantastic!).

Two boxes sit on top of sand;
a curtain is draped on chairs;
a hand appears to float in air,
in front of puzzled stares.

A coil of rope lies limp on cubes,
while a mirror reflects a cat;
a turtle sits atop a sink,
beneath a feathered hat.

These men and women of artistic bent
outdo each other to provoke,
with metaphors all juxtaposed,
and too deep for ordinary folk.

So, to get our attention and stimulate thought,
a poet or prophet may appear;
but instead of instructing or offering insights,
too many just merit a jeer.

Lighten Up

HA-HA! HA-HA! HA-HA! HA!
and HO-HO! HO-HO: HO!
We laugh at jokes that tickle us:
for nature has made us so.

A joke is what just breaks the ice
of serious sober talk,
and makes one smile or guffaw loud:
our gift from birthing's stork!

"Did you hear the one...", so starts a joke,
and our eyes begin to brighten:
prepared for a little mirth or twist,
in hopes our burdens lighten.

It may be loud or just a smile
that greets a witty joke;
but our laughter eases sober thoughts
when covered with humor's cloak.

So, make me laugh or at least crack a smile,
for it breaks that serious edge.
Separate me from humdrum life
with a really humorous wedge!

Re-Lived

In memory's mists, those ancient times,
I often return to peek:
and reacquaint myself again
with these images about which I speak.

Those were innocent and carefree times
that bound my growing years;
when play and streets all helped to mold,
surrounded by my peers.

Enmeshed in mind scenes come to fore,
imaged pictures real:
with playland's streets and snowball fights
'til mamma called for meal!

The hand-cranked 2-cent merry-go-round
brought solace and escape,
as did the penny candy store
or birthday's ribbon crepe.

We loved our skates and marbles, too,
in spite of weather windy.
We'd look up until we saw a plane
and then we'd all shout , "LINDY!".

Stick and stoop ball gave me joy,
the hide and seek, as well.
And kick-the can made metal fly.
My, such times were swell!

I can't forget the cry in yards
of "I will buy old clothes!",
or bottled milk on window sills
with tops of cream that froze.

What I recall most of those old days
were men with tongs and hooks and pick,
who climbed four flights to deliver ice.
I cannot forget that trick!

Another remembered common sight
was when washed clothes needed drying.
They used two pulleys, clothes pins and line.
There were laundries, but we weren't buying.

The streets were barren of the car,
instead the horse was king,
pulling wagons of vegetables,
and we heard the peddlers sing:

"If you have money, come down and buy!
if not, stay up and cry!".
"It's fresh and ripe so save a dime!".
He was a loud, impressive guy!

I can't forget the push-cart stoves,
with charcoal, fire and stack,
that sold delicious knish or beans…
The thought just takes me back!

The radio was my trusty friend.
My heroes told such tales:
if memory serves, Buck Rogers flew
and the Lone Ranger never fails!

Girls were girls, and we were boys.
Our world was unlike theirs.
They jumped with ropes and played with Jacks,
un-alike as grapes and pears.

continued...

They played with dolls and avoided boys
(we avoided them as well!).
They played hop-scotch and played at "house"
...two worlds as you can tell!

Nothing matched our Saturday's escapes
when at the movies we spent time.
There's never been an equal since,
and it only cost a dime!

All week we waited to take our seats,
the crowd of kids like me,
to spend four hours in dark escape:
just why, I think you'll see.

We saw two pictures: "A" and "B",
a newsreel and two cartoons,
a serial episode that left you panting,
and we left with eyes in ruins.

On top of that they'd give a gift,
as if they didn't give enough.
The day was long, so we brought our lunch.
Oh, all our lives were rough!

With new shoes you'd get a pencil box,
even one with drawer;
with every haircut came a ball:
such memories you can't ignore.

I leave lots out as I reminisce,
for who can re-live a past?
Those days were full and honey-sweet,
as long as memories last.

Wishful Thinking

However small a dog's tail is
it makes its thoughts quite clear:
like metronome beat or a waving fan
he's happy when you're near.

The sheer delight when the errand's done
and he sees you once again,
making clear his patient love for you,
beyond a poet's pen.

It's a jealous sight to see such scenes
when we have our spirits sag.
It would be nice if friends and love
would, too, have tails to wag!

A Young Man's Song

What is my fate, what paths to take,
which mate will cherish me?
Will I bow to king or queen,
a beggar or chieftain be?

Will politic's call envelop me,
or inventions make me rich?
Will travel be my destiny,
or the army for a hitch?

My plan to write that cherished book:
is that a useless dream?
Will I live to my golden years,
or join a winning team?

Such questions pulse within my mind
and long to know the score.
Will I marry once for keeps
or marry three or four?

These riddles burn for answers clear,
but I'm told just where to go
to get advice from those who know,
if just I have the dough.

Their visions' gifts and guiding hands
are just the tools I need
to know the future and its course
and warning signs to heed.

The fortune teller's crystal ball,
the reader of my palm,
the tea leaf reader's expert eyes
should provide my puzzle's balm.

The astrologer's skill sees far, they say,
and peels away the veil.
The Chinese fortune cookies, too,
will warn me of the gale.

So, here I am, a blowing leaf,
in need of sightings clear.
I hope to learn what lies ahead:
that's what I want to hear.

But nothing's sure and can't be guessed,
it's silly to have fear,
I'll try my luck and trust my fate
and play it all by ear.

Soft Sell

Every ad that seeks to sell,
whatever that may be,
has learned the trick that seems to work
and makes for selling's key.

Every person in an ad
displays a smiling face,
to lure you into a friendly frame
that invites a sale's embrace.

Of course, you say, what did you expect,
some frowning, cheerless guy,
with rasping voice and stubble beard
inviting you to buy?

So, when next you see a call to buy,
be aware of purpose's plan;
resist the smile and look instead
at the hand of the ad man!

Walking Books

Every person you may meet
or see upon the street,
has stories that would make eyes shine,
of victories or defeat.

Events in lives provide such tales
of loss and sorrow, too:
of friends and kin alive or gone,
all contribute to the brew.

The happy times and dangers faced,
the loves and joys or pain,
adventures, travel, faltering times
and energies spent in vain.

So look again at passers-by
and see instead of strangers,
a trove of stories that may bewitch
from meek to wild Lone Rangers.

One cannot tell with cursory glance
the victors from the losers,
not dress or sturdy step or pace
tells chosen from the choosers.

This makes the mystery very deep,
with imagining all we know.
It's fun to match the sight with guess
of elusive Janes or Joe.

Favoritism

A dog and cat are different folks,
ask any owner's view.
A cat is regal, slinky, proud,
a loner loving few.

No excitement seems to stir
the creature's self-control.
It eyes the fish, the birds and mice
and plays its haughty role.

Its tail is long and held in check
with no emotion shown.
Its enigmatic eyes will tell
he'd rather be alone.

He accepts you as a useful friend
who feeds and provides his needs;
he's a patrician, sulky, introvert
and typical of his breed.

I admit that he can be unique,
a personality,
who may just rub against your leg
but then says "Let me be!"

The dog, however, will tie a knot
of friendship, close and dear,
with frisky, lively playful moods,
whenever you are near.

He'll jump and catch an object thrown
and bark with joy when pleased,
especially when you appear in sight
or when he's simply teased.

He can't conceal a hidden thought,
for all his feelings show.
He's playful, friendly as can be.
His tail will let you know!

He'll roll right over for a belly scratch
with eyes just glazed with thanks;
compared to cats a dog relates;
I'm with dog owners' ranks.

Now, cats are cute, I admit as much;
I'm respectful in my talks.
But, by now it's clear which pet's for me
if not for those daily walks!

Hello, It's Me

We cannot get too far from friends,
they must know where we are,
and what we ate and how we feel,
when walking or in a car.

There's fear that grips some needy souls,
that urge to talk and patter,
that need to stay in touch and chat:
we listeners just don't matter!

They need an extra arm to hold
that magic wireless phone.
It's time for Nature to respond
and make us an octopus clone!

I don't refer to needed calls
for messages and such;
such calls are usually very short,
so I don't mind them as much.

It's fun to note this need to share
and need to share it all:
to join your day with other phones
and think who next to call.

The streets are strange to watch these days,
pedestrians absorbed with self:
with continual social needs to meet,
or the alternative lonely shelf!

With voices heard from near and far,
you look to see who's there,
disturbing my tranquility,
for silence is so rare!

Years ago, in ages past,
if someone talked to air
while walking along a crowded way
they'd be sent for urgent care!

On bus or train, just anywhere,
it could be store or mall,
that chatter sound just makes me mad
...unless I make that call!

A Bombardier's Story

Mission is posted…I scan with my light,
flying tomorrow…can't drink much tonight.
No time to roll 'em…must hit the sack.
(I'll probably dream of fighters and flak.)

The plane is too heavy…the runway too short,
The air is a bronco…with hiss and with snort,
My mask is too leaky…no map is aboard,
My fingers are frozen…I've forgotten my cord.

I toss and I turn…the I.P.'s ahead,
The sky is afire…I mumble with dread.
An engine is smoking…oh, hell, what a fix.
Then a nudge and a voice and "Briefing's at six!"

My eyes are so tired, my blanket's so warm;
Aw, gee, I'm not eager…why doesn't it storm?
I squint at the darkness – it's all gloom and chills.
It requires an effort…the strongest of wills!

I trudge to the mess hall…still half asleep,
fall into a foxhole, bump into a jeep.
At last I sit down…it's French toast, darn the luck,
I haven't much time…I must catch the truck.

Still chewing and gulping, gun at my side,
I bounce and I tremble…Oh Lord, what a ride!
The ruts and the holes…maybe mud and a splash;
the road is the bomb run, each jolt is a crash.

With squeal of the brakes, I jump to my feet,
run down the steps…look around for a seat.
Shaken and winded, briefing begins,
I look at the map, wondering, Vienna or Linz?

The meeting has started...I sit back and sigh
and murmur "If this were the last one to fly...
if blue were the heavens...and bombing no more,
an end to the maiming....the blood and the gore.

"If men could be human and decent and free,
with God in their souls...like roots to a tree,
if we could be home...oh, peace would be grand..."
A shrug...and I turn to the business at hand.

"Maximum effort...we're leading today.
The Skipper himself is to show us the way...".
The Major is droning... I peer through the smoke;
visibility is zero...I cough and I choke.

I wheeze and I sneeze...while S-2 reports.
I whine and I whimper...while "Weather" cavorts.
Eight-tenths is "no buono"... "Aw, nuts!" someone cries,
but we're crammed full of data...words from the wise.

We rush for the door..."Hubba.-hubba" our song,
My thoughts are of clouds....J hope they're not wrong.
We're soon on our way.... jammed in the truck;
somebody yells "Wire!", I just barely duck!

The wind wets my eyes. I quake and I quiver.
Oh, miserable day....I jounce and I shiver.
We arrive at the shack...alight with a groan,
grab all our stuff ....and grumble and moan.

We stop...and suddenly upturn our eyes;
we bellow and cheer...two flares fill the skies!
"It's back to the sack" we all shout with glee;
we laugh and we jump...like drunks on a spree.

What a commotion...ol' Fate and her jests!
Off come the chutes, the suits and mae wests.
Our mission is finished.... "Hey, let's go to town!"
This'll never win wars...but bless the stand-down!

I Give Up!

Today's a day I'd rather forget!
The devil was picking on me!
I bit my tongue and stubbed my toe,
and couldn't find my car key!

I awoke with a headache after a restless night,
waking after a bout of tossing:
still shaking from a frightful dream
about stalling on a railroad crossing.

No toothpaste was left, and there was no hot water;
the toilet refused to flush.
Still sleeplessly groggy with the day barely started,
I felt like some overhung lush.

The next thing I knew I burnt my eggs,
and the toast had a charcoal look.
The coffee tasted like vinegar,
and I discovered the phone off the hook.

The mail brought a notice for darn jury duty,
and bills I'd forgotten to pay.
I tripped on the stairway on my way out:
it seemed like a comical play!

So, on and on, my day inched along,
which included my dog wetting my rug.
But the day wasn't over, it wasn't to be:
my slippery hand broke my mug.

With the day halfway through and my fingers all crossed,
I was waiting to see what was next!
I had read many books on maintaining calm,
but reality overwhelmed such text!

I next lost my wallet with my identity card,
and had not a clue as to where.
But, if the person who found it is willing to risk it,
they're welcome to be me, if they dare!

Rambling

I feel like Walter Mitty
living in a city
which is very gritty
and not so itty-bitty,
which reminds me of a ditty
which is so witty
but I can't recall it,
and that's a pity.

I have a hunch
I shouldn't munch
before I have lunch,
with milk or punch
unless it's brunch,
and for your advice,
thanks a bunch.

There once was a fellow called Shorty,
who enjoyed a life quite sporty.
His skills were self-taughty
and he liked being naughty
until he got caughty
doing things which he hadn't oughty.

Still More Rambling

There once was a girl called Sadie,
who was anything but a lady;
she was tough and rough,
her voice was gruff,
and she never was afraidy.
Until one day she sassed her mom,
from whom she learned her lessons,
who proved that sass will never pass
painful woodshed sessions.

~ ~ ~

There once was a cook named Mark,
who went to the park after dark,
and peeled a tree,
when no one would see,
and tried to make soup out of bark.

He added some juice
from the neck of a goose,
and bone from the tail of a moose;
added pepper and salt,
but didn't know when to halt,
so he threw in the knot of a noose.

The diners went wild, no protests were filed,
the dish became known far and wide.
Other cooks around town
gave Mark a crown,
and stripped every tree of its hide.

Shy Companion

A shadow is a strange friend,
or a silent, relentless stalker;
following your every move, going wherever you go.
Sometimes it is in front, leading you on
and pointing the way.
Other times behind, following like a faithful dog.

But an odd thing can be noticed:
it is totally afraid of light,
and will always seek to hide from it.
If the light is in front of you,
it will run behind you.
If the light is in the back,
it will run to the front.
The same is true on either the left
or right of you, for it will always
run and hide from the light.

It also has this trick:
it will completely disappear
if the light comes from above.

It is very odd.

Keep It Clean

In the vernacular, a gambler,
if successful, can clean up!
With no luck, he gets taken
to the cleaners.
It's a dirty business!

If unsuccessful, one is all washed up,
or wiped out!
If asking for a loan,
it often is "No soap!"
"Confess! Come clean!" the police might say.

Airing dirty linen in public
is not nice.

Politicians often launder the truth.
I don't know any dirty jokes!
The reporter got the dirt
on the mayor.
He washed his hands
of the whole thing.
It was a clean get-away!

Grime does not pay!
It will all come out
in the wash! As it is said.

SOLUTION

So many ways to hurt and kill
we hear about each day:
religion, land, no matter what,
is there no other way?

The ills, the maimed, the homes destroyed;
is there no end in sight?
In name of God or fanatic's cause,
is there no way but fight?

Wouldn't it be a peaceful world
if brother loved his brother,
and instead of strife we learned to say:
"Neah! Neah! and you're another!"

Choices

The winner's circle is indeed quite small,
for few fellows have made it to the top.
Our presidents reflect our changing times,
and range from the great and the flop.

Our national needs and changing moods
call forth the proper one to lead;
we've been lucky with many of the choices made,
but sad with the unsavory deed.

It's hard to find wisdom in those we elect
who can help steer our ship of state
through shoals and impediments here and abroad,
so only a rare few can be called great.

Mt. Rushmore, of course, still honors just four
to remind us of examples we've found.
We get what we deserve and deserve what we get,
as we respond to our future's sound.

RETRIEVAL

One day there may be a way
to download a brain's gray:
its accumulated wisdom hoard,
its knowledge, memories, whatever's stored,
which, otherwise, would be lost and gone.
It's a novel idea to ponder upon.

Void

I never knew my father well,
We never spoke at all.
He was a stranger in my home,
between us was a wall.

We ate and did our separate things,
there was no talk or fun.
His face was glum with harried look.
I was a strange man's son.

He came a loner to this land,
I'm sure it was a stress
to find a place, a job to do
and find a wife, I guess.

I hold no grudge, he did work hard.
He didn't drink or roam.
He never joked or even smiled.
He made a lifeless home.

What memories linger of this past
that dwell on him and me,
still haunt and cause unease and hurt…
I have to let it be.

Mia And Dvd

The DDS and our MD
will join the Ph.D.
The MFA and MIA
will meet with FCC.

The AAA knows MPH
and gives the SOS.
The CBS and NBC
I watch with PBS.

The PS at the letter's end,
a jaunty FDR
speaking on the radio
to counter DAR.

It's FOB and DNA,
GI and USO;
the NYPD keeps the peace,
BMW is for show.

AC,DC moves the world,
TNT is TKO.
The VP needs some TLC
to counter a UFO.

A PFC is a POW,
DDT is bad.
The FBI taps your phone
and VD makes you sad.

The BLT is good for lunch,
And OJ just as well.
The GOP and VCR,
I have LP's to sell.

Before AD there was BC,
TVA was good.
But FYI it's SRO,
so stand up if you could.

Your IQ in the USA
can match a CPA.
FM sounds good on QXR,
the FCC should stay.

Get that CAT scan and MRI
and learn that CPR;
LA's the place with SUV's
and EU is way too far.

Thank goodness for FDIC,
but watch that PCB.
At MIT and NYU
a few can go for free.

We watch the S & P real close,
the CEOs are smart.
The IPO's no IBM,
is this a rich man's start?

Of HDL and LDL
you've got to be aware;
for NASA and the NFL,
each would likely care.

To join the MVP parade,
the RBI's OK.
The PC helps with your ID
and has the final say.

It's 8 AM and PM's time
to take the RX med,
and watch TV and DVD
and so PJ's and bed.

Awaited News

Every day brings break-through news
of our genetic and basic selves,
filling our questioning knowledge voids,
such as who will be giants or elves.

We're learning about our drives and traits,
and our brain's power to think.
There's been progress, too, as we read again
of the search for the missing link.

We know of girls' pattern of playing with dolls;
instinct and nurture are seen.
But I patiently await the sought-after find
of the boys' elusive wheel gene.

Exit

It is a hard concept to accept,
that of our body's exit:
taking with it all identity,
markings, memories, ranking
and potentials.

The new void, which our body once filled,
thins the immensity
of those remaining, providing a residue
of thought for the others who will, inevitably,
later follow.

No mortal life is a waste,
but an influence and memory to somebody.

Life's cauldron is fed and emptied,
in an endless drama, through eternity.

Our Winter's Tale

In each of us a novel lies
awaiting pen and pad.
Our story's plot is ours alone:
the bad, the mad, the sad.

It could be, too, a happy plot
that may be worth a smile,
of early youth and memory's play
that sits in our brains' file.

The home recalled as we grew up,
our pets and window's views;
the places lived from then to now,
and things that still amuse.

We might not be aware of this,
but of this we may be sure,
in our minds our movies play,
our scenes will long endure.

Our parent's love or sad neglect
helped guide us well or not.
Our siblings' lives blend closely, too,
to help create our plot.

So play and school and work all blend
to make us who we are.
Adventures fill our background screen;
we all have travelled far.

We think of joy which good times brought,
when all went well as hoped:
our winning hands as luck joined us;
when not, we somehow coped.

Our growing years were linked to fate,
from jobs to love to mates.
Our chapters speak with blood and tears:
no one forgets those dates.

Of course there were some happy days
(we grin when we recall);
laugh times just mingle with the sad:
we rise as well as fall.

We've lost good friends, we've made some more,
our fashions came and went.
We've seen it all, been through our hells,
our spirits, we hope, unbent.

Our chapters tell our unique plots,
our imprints mark each page.
Our storied clash with life is told
as bumbling fool or sage.

So, slowly pass our days and years,
we make our way with care,
our varied tales will chapters make.
Life's ride was paid our fare.

As gray and creaks engulf our lot,
our lives are not yet done.
We're still around (thank God for that!).
It's been a busy run.

City Song

The chirping crickets and circling hawks
oversee their terrains
and announce, indisputably,
give-no-quarter presences
and a sobering contrast
to the city's cemented, bricked
and girded over-dwelled and bustling
and stark counterpoint,
like a Niagara of ceaseless, frothy,
rumbling power, daily swallowing
the unwary and the weak,
the timid and the luckless:
somebody's continuous puzzle and challenge
to subsist, overcome,
escape, or triumph.

The transportation exertions,
the city sounds and neons,
are not natural ones,
but the ongoing residue and ambiance
of the herded and denizens
coping, repairing, shopping,
transporting, delivering, parading,
vending, erranding, servicing:
the unnatural counter-equivalents
of scurrying ants
or the bee-buzzing of the hive,
and all under a blanket of accompanying dust
and being sirened to death.

The rituals of living make one thankful
for a park, tree, bush, bench
or alcove of quiet:
and the time or leisure to enjoy it.

Book Learning

A know-it-all with printed leaves
humbly hides and patiently awaits
to live its purpose…
as dictionary.

Puppy Love

Those friends, co-habitants, companions called pets,
provide solace and warmth and much more.
They fill personal voids and ask for no more
than awaiting the key in the door.

Their feeding and attending to natural calls
are costs accepted as par.
The puppies and dogs fill niches in life;
the rewards exceed payment by far.

The signs of acceptance are so plain to see,
this bonding effect so real.
It's a familial addition, an aging together:
personalities each sharing a deal.

Some names spring to mind and memories touch:
There's Barley and Sugar and Harry,
Queeny and Louie and Tootsy and Rex;
and we can't overlook sweet Larry.

They give all they are able to give and then some.
Their entrance and exit leave marks,
Time is enriched as we all age together,
with the music of whine and of barks.

Balm

All in all, it might be worse,
even if hurt or ill.
Whatever came our way unplanned
is better than the Devil's grill.

A glance around just proves the point:
somewhere there's worse to bear.
We sympathize and cluck our tongue:
compare plights, if you dare.

For most of us, we can bear our lot,
despite a dent or crack.
This too shall pass, you've heard it said:
so go forward and don't look back!

And I Approve This Message!

My opponent is a well-known slob
unwashed behind his ears.
He embezzled money from his firm,
and has been drunk for years.

He's a crook who won't admit his guilt,
and likes to fondle kids.
He lies and cheats and cooks the books,
and submits phony bids.

He slapped his wife in public once,
embarrassing his friends.
She sued for divorce that very day.
He confuses means and ends.

This is the man who wants your votes;
he'll promise you the moon.
If he's your next elected choice,
he'll bring us certain ruin!

He's stolen once, he will again.
He's on the take for sure.
He'll vote the way his backers want,
His dishonesty will make us poor!

He loves to be with lobbyists,
who entertain and dine.
They write the laws with sport and trips.
He'll rank zero from one to nine.

He's dumb and thinks the earth is flat
and the poor deserve their lot,
and the world was made in one week's time
and the planet was meant to be hot!

He represents the worst in men,
who could not care less for you.
If his party and his sponsors win,
democracy is gone from view.

So, don't believe his lying ads,
he is no friend of yours!
His smiling face and glib remarks
conceal the world of whores.

Musing

The world as we know it is changing so fast
I feel like a little lost child.
I still write with a quill by a kerosene lamp,
and so far won't be beguiled.

We got along fine, our horses were smart;
they pulled and plowed and were loved.
But along came seats that rode on four wheels
and away from our world we were shoved.

The phones that were cranked were good for our arms,
although everyone knew when we spoke.
The canning we did and ice that cooled food:
oh, what memories these evoke!

Over the years, to make a long story short,
the life as we knew it was gone;
our lamps morphed into little glass bulbs.
I won't tell what happened to our john.

There are so many changes that others may admire,
making living more easy to endure.
But whatever these smart kids can think of and invent,
there's still value in the old ways, for sure!

Applause

What a curious expression of delight
and appreciation
is the act and sound
of palms attacking one another
in a most unfriendly way.
The more the appreciation,
the more furious,
the aggressive noise of battle.

Inflated Fun

From our earliest years, what delighted us so,
was the thrill of remembered balloons;
those round and colorful fantasies on strings
suspended like so many moons.

Over our heads and dancing with the breeze,
they were escapes from where we were:
to a fairy place which we held tightly aloft.
Even today, our memories stir.

And if, by chance, one left our clutch
and rose up into the sky,
we felt such loss and emptiness
and just tried not to cry.

They were our friends from another world:
floating things of joy.
They were such fun against the dull
for either girl or boy.

Now, adding shapes and words and such,
comic characters, too,
distorts the memory of my younger times.
I just don't like what's new.

And let's not forget today's floating giants,
monsters in parades.
I prefer the simple unadorned:
the rest is just charades.

Primitive Art

There's creativity in every group,
where the expressive ones reside:
those special folks among their peers,
whose talents won't be denied.

They weave and paint and carve and build;
their colors just brighten life.
They dance and sing and sculpt with clay,
to counter strain and strife.

They ornament and decorate
with feathers, skins or wood.
They use whatever tools there are:
their skills are really good.

Head dress, fabrics, jewelry, too,
reflect, some artist's vision.
There were composers of rhythm and sound
(I'm guessing without critics' derision.)

So, the artists live and cultures thrive,
regardless of time or age.
We like to call it "primitive"
but who are we to gauge?

How Do I Love Me?
(A Braggart's Voice)

So let me count the ways, my friends,
I know my way around.
I look upon my charm and face
and hear success's sound.

My mind is keen and filled with guile,
my hair is full and dark.
I live by cleverness and wits.
Our differences are stark.

The least I do makes happy days,
I get the most I can.
I follow hard the money's lure
...I am that sort of man.

I want fine things and want some more
of clothing silk and wool,
of fashion's best and gadgets new:
I cannot get my full.

I'm smart and sharp (and know I am,)
most others are but fools.
They know much less than my keen brain,
they simply follow rules.

Because of what myself deserves
all others will provide.
I know the ways that smartness knows:
self-interest is my guide.

So ask me now how I love me
(you cannot win my game):
the most for least and play for fun
God's special is my name!

I play and eat the best with wine
(you can't compete with me!).
Let others pay and watch me smirk…
Now, don't you all agree?

There are three words that well describe
(I could, you know, name nine).
I'm one of those that fill this world
with me, myself and mine!

Flow

My mind races along a changing thought
as an emerging picture colorfully flashes
on the snowy boughs and limbs of
yesteryear's youth.

What years have shrouded in veily
mists of time and tide now expose
themselves in memory's grip.

Homes and friends and seasons pass
along the well-traveled trail
of backward glance of reunions
locked deep in aging's embrace.

My mother's grip is tightly binding
as formative agent and history's glue
and with visions of trials and soups
and selfless love and pride,
and lying dormant on our inexorable path
to here and now, but springs to life
by the mirrored glass of quiet memory.

The play and faces of ghosts and games
form vaporous imagery, leavened by
seasons' march to now.

Names and hearths fill the void of time
as opening doors let in the slumbering past,
and retro-life merges with the present.

Sorrow's weeping kept silenced and checked
relives itself as backward memory's
frightened youth puzzles and weeps.

Light and dark alternate forever with visions
of quiet movement slipping past
and leaping over ruts and stones as muscles
harden and life's moving creeks carry
spores of meaning to their changing destinations.

Sadness somehow follows such a re-living
for what has left and cannot be retrieved
(except in contemplative review by ourselves);
for when we cease, our
residual past will form the dust
inhaled by our saddened heirs.

In turn, in their own reposed and silent moments
our replayed images will form the vapors
of nostalgic reveries, for them.

Laugh

What gears in our creature machine
produce a giggle
and such peculiar sounds
of laughter unique to us alone?
Is it, indeed, a "funny bone"?

Continuity

This pictured parental pair
who gave birth and life
has missed the blooming fruit
of their unioned time,
as memory's spool unwinds,
and gazes are exchanged in silence.

Their framed and stiffened faces
eye us solemnly from eras gone,
and help bridge the gap
from then to now.
In turn, our own portrait images will join
the parading past to remind others
of our own passing by.

Respect

The lonely weed we seek to kill
is nature's child as well.
We try to rid it from our view:
it's worth is hard to sell.

The name bespeaks an underclass
of meritless waste of space,
destroying planted charm and plan,
like homespun versus lace.

It has its right to grow and thrive
but gardeners don't agree.
They try to rid it from their sight,
away from plant and tree.

I do not wish their feelings hurt,
poor sorrowful orphan kin,
with equal rights from seedlings on,
their plaudits we can win.

I wish to make amends, you see,
by giving them their due
and planting only weeds despite
their lack of scent or hue.

In such a weedy garden patch,
if any flower grew,
we'd pull the roots and say "Be gone!"
and weeds would say "Thank you!".
So, dandelions, crab grass all:
you have a spokesman true.
You fill each crack and cranny width,
but you're God's children too!

Stand your ground and hold head high,
you're here as good as they;
ignore the sneers and killer drugs,
you're here and will always stay!

I'm for the underdog, you see,
soft-hearted as can be,
for those left out and also shunned,
now, don't you all agree?

A Short Biography

I was just a little boy back then
just starting out in life;
(it was quite a hop and skip ahead
before I had a wife!)

I played, I learned, and had my friends
who made me laugh and giggle.
I also met the mean and tough
whose presence made me wiggle.

My world back then was full and fun,
I jumped and ran and biked.
I listened to the radio
at programs that I liked.

My school was there to teach me things
and meet with those like me.
So far there was no hint at all
of what was yet to be.

With growth my clothes no longer fit,
my pets just come and go.
I saw my family's ups and downs.
I just went with the flow.

As years go by and birthday candles
burn on many cakes,
I learn that living as I'd wish
consists of gives and takes.

I noticed that in Fortune's world
there are many left behind:
some get the juice and enjoy the taste,
while others get the rind.

I did the best with what I had
with talent, nerve and brain.
The race was on to make our lives
and to survive the strain.

I watched the world just come apart
as tyrants had their way.
What was our fate if we stood by?
Your guess or mine can't say.

So, fought, I did, until we won
and helped to see some peace,
which still eludes our world today,
so troubles never cease.

I married and we raised two girls,
whose lives fill us with pride.
I take my place as senior now,
and look back at the ride.

The newer little boys like me
who've gone on their own roads,
will follow their own destinies
and carry life's new loads.

ONE AND ONLY

The earth is one in interlocking harmony
and delicate balance,
an intricate, living and
pulsating creation:
a floating speck of mysterious origin
and unknown demise.

New Year's Gracious Company

What elàn and verve as evening moves
beyond the forks and spoons,
and cake and beans and fish delicious
ending in croons and tunes!

How splendidly close and warm and sweet
this group comes close to being...
as years and age roar past the clock
unshackling curbs and freeing.

The icy chills of stymied thrusts
preventing forward leaping;
let leaders lead and followers grope,
all friends in our God's keeping.

Building Blocks

A	B	C	D	
	E	F	G	
H	I	J	K	
L	M	N	O	P
Q	R	S	T	
U	V	W		
X	Y	Z		

With these letters I am smitten:
They form all words spoken and written
and are the ingredients for alphabet soup.

It's true, but also hard to believe,
that with these 26 letters we can weave
all the poetry and books we enjoy.

And So It Is Written

I cannot but wonder and guess story's end
whenever I see scratched in cement,
the young puppy love signs of initials and heart
and if I should rejoice or lament.

The blood is so warm and love overwhelms
(we've all been there before):
the romantic yearning and dreaming and wish
for the opening of reciprocal's door.

It's usually the boy who scratches the lines,
(I seem to remember I did),
to let the world share his hope and his love,
a permanent message from a kid.

And how, indeed, do such stories end,
and did she respond to his heart?
Or was she aloof and express her own love
and scratch her own sidewalk art?

Remembered

Crouching behind memory's bramble and bush
within his forested brain,
lay hidden and silent the young man's thoughts
of his mother's death and its pain.

He hadn't cried since infancy's times
but tears wet his eyes and cheek,
as relatives strove to soothe his pain
that day, so sad and so bleak.

Her face was so peaceful in her final boxed home,
lipsticked and powdered for gazing;
her various ills now masked by peace,
the result of neglect and aging.

She was kind, hard-working and strived to be good
and provided a clean, stable home.
She was there to tend and feed and protect:
and deserving quite more than a poem.

She came as an immigrant girl from abroad,
sent off with a prayer and some hope,
found work and made do with patience and trials
and found someone to share and to cope.

She was gentle and loving and blessed with her child,
the one who now weeps at the loss.
She gave comfort and caring without holding back,
and now joins the grass and the moss.

Seasons

We've learned to meet those seasons four,
and enjoy each one, in turn,
as each year unfolds in monthly pace
enabling us to learn.

The winter shows its frosty face
and surely leads to spring,
when all awake from slumber's rest,
preparing for summer's fling.

Then, there's fall to usher in
the winter's start again.
Our years keep pace as best we can;
the question is: 'til when?

Fortune's Twist

I knew him by the name of Jeff,
I had seen him now and then.
He liked to chat and had no airs.
He walked a dog called Ben.

We spoke when we met in town one day
and he needed a friendly ear.
We saw a bench and settled in,
while Ben just hovered near.

He told a tale of happier times,
his days as a circus clown.
He was a star and played to crowds
until destiny let him down.

It seems that Ben co-starred with him
as an important part of the act.
He jumped through hoops and rolled around.
Every night, the tent was packed.

But fortune had a twist in store
that shook the comfort tree.
He fell in love with a circus girl
with a story hard to foresee.

The girl Jeff loved had a cat named Rose,
sullen, gray and mean.
Whenever it encountered Ben
the result was a hellish scene.

When Ben came near, Rose hissed and screeched;
Ben's sight caused fur to fly.
Rosie spit and leaped, and scratched to kill.
Jeff feared that Ben would die.

The famous act that brought Jeff fame,
in which Ben starred as well,
was doomed, it seemed, if this cat and dog
would be where the lovers dwelled.

Neither one would part with pets,
the tug of love no match;
to part was sad but better than
an acrobat's missed catch.

We each have tales to share or not
of sad or sunny times.
When Jeff and Ben walk by again,
I'll think of these few rhymes.

Funny

I wonder what jokes made the ancients laugh.
Did cavemen giggle and grunt?
Did isolated native tribes share humor
to accompany a serious hunt?

Did the sound of laughter break the gloom
at some hairy jokester's pun?
Was there some comic in cave or hut
who had a sense of fun?

I can imagine those early men in the wild
with clubs or stones and spears,
gathered around a smoking fire
telling jokes to dispel their fears.

I can hear one say, "There were these guys..."
or another say, "Did you hear the one...?"
Such mirth might bring a smile or two
or cause the teller to run!

Is humor a natural human trait
along with the others we know?
I think it was meant to ease the strain
of living's drudge and woe.

So, what we know of primitive life
is really not complete
until we learn if they're like us.
Now, wouldn't that be neat!

Vista

With a giant's view
sitting atop the shoulders
of a paternal pedestal,
a lucky child holds court
with previewed growth
and giggles away with every step.

Some Nerve!

I thumb my nose at dumb requests,
my shoulders sometimes I shrug.
I wink at fate while ankle deep in despair
and my earlobe I simply just tug.

I forgive and I turn my other cheek
and I have to hand it to you.
Don't belly-ache, but take it on the chin;
you'll be much happier when you do!

I'm all thumbs, it seems, from time to time
but I try to stay on my toes.
I swallow hard when I do anything wrong,
for it's not as if anything goes.

To amuse the kids and make them laugh
my funny face is a twist.
The kids tickle my fancy (wherever that is!)
and I punish with a slap on the wrist.

You said a mouthful, I so often say,
to get it off my chest.
I scratch my head in bewilderment,
and it's tongue-in-cheek when I jest.

What makes my skin crawl, I want it to be known,
are those who are a pain in the butt:
who don't foot the bill and have some real gall
who brow-beat, and love to just strut.

My body gives voice, as you can see from the above.
It's funny how much we depend
on our own body parts to help express and describe
and stick out our neck for a friend.

Some words just stick in my throat when I speak,
my brow just furrows in thought.
I have backbone when needed. Some things I can't stomach.
And some things just cannot be bought!

When you speak I'm all ears, for I know you're all heart;
you'll never elbow your way through a crowd.
I'd fight tooth and nail to help you succeed;
You're brainy and you'll do yourself proud.

Wishes

I know them not. They don't know me,
yet sugary kindness flows.
For when I go to shop or buy,
I meet friendly Janes and Joes.

The clouds may burst with downpour's gray,
the heat may simmer toes.
The cold may numb, the sun may broil
yet some words banish woes

My purchase made, my duties done,
as I am heading towards the door,
I hear that parting friendly wish
that shakes me to my core.

Some words amuse and light my mood
when hearing someone say
those caring, trite and charming words
like "Have a nice day!"

Expression

Mall and small and said and dread
and some things odoriferous,
or sad and glad and whale and tale,
or thought's metamorphosis:
Oh, what to do when writing poems
with style's selectivity,
to rhyme or not in meter's thrall,
avoiding ambiguity.

Rhyming speaks lustre and skill to be read
as a game of challenge and wit;
but a poet's preferred choices are equally valid,
if some mind's fire is lit.

Oh, Captain, my Captain or road less traveled,
or a poem lovely as a tree,
all ring true with equal thought and emotion,
which should be enough for you and me.

All verse can reveal with metaphor and allusion
the depth of a mind or an eye;
the skill of the rhyme is not needed to observe
the truth of our life and the lie:
to see and to feel and relate to our world
with mirth or merely a sigh.

Our visions and feelings we so wish to express,
our comings and goings, as well.
Our encounters, so strange, and our insights and thoughts
we simply must write, share and tell.

Forgotten

He stands upon a pedestal,
his name carved into stone,
forgotten although big as life
upon whom once fortune shone.

Pigeons rest upon his head,
fallen leaves in the fall.
He was a hero in his time;
just why I can't recall.

A governor, orator or army general,
his fame deserted now,
reminds us of the moving stage
and the short-lived actor's bow.

The eras pass and take their tales
but leave their heroes here.
I wonder how our own statued names
will puzzle future's peer.

Preference

I can't help but be gushy and happy to be
where the snows and blizzards don't come,
and no howling winds and ice on the street:
I'm so glad, you can bet, and then some!

Such weather is not now a friend of mine,
I can't stand frozen fingers and ears;
the skidding and sliding and pipes that are frozen
that I've endured for uncountable years.

When young, I enjoyed the skis and snow fights,
the snowmen with hat and a pipe;
the icicles that dangled from eaves and the trees.
Back then there was no reason to gripe.

But age yearns for warmth and calming blue skies,
and walks with the sun and light breeze;
where colorful shirts and shorts that we wear
thumb noses at the word "freeze" !

My bones demand kindness and are beginning to creak,
they've served me well and are friends.
I owe them repayment for years of support
and together we'll enjoy time 'til ours ends.

I Thought You'd Want To Know

I have opinions, slogans and personal likes,
favorite candidates, too:
advice to offer wherever I go,
and I'm willing to share this with you!

Wherever I go my politics follow,
my favorite team, as well;
even my religion is your's to see.
There's nothing I cannot tell!

I want you to know my school and sport.
There's no chance for you to bicker.
I'll even slow down to make it easy for you
to appreciate my bumper sticker!

Even my rear window is a billboard to see
what I think or where I'm from.
I'll share and be frank, just wanting to be friendly:
I have so much to tell and then some.

Homage

There are so many sports that depend on a ball
for pleasure and such fun to keep score,
whether baseball, football, soccer or golf,
and I think I can name a few more.

There's handball, ping pong, tennis and squash,
basketball, volleyball, too;
and bowling, billiards (or pool as we say):
for the athlete, there's plenty to do.

There's marbles, skeeball, cricket and rugby,
polo, both in water and on horse;
jai-alai, or hi-li, and croquet on the lawn
and racquetball and field hockey, of course.

So, it's throw and catch and sociable play,
with little or no time to rest:
softball, beach ball, stoopball and stick,
and the effort for personable best!

Let's include bocce, cricket and lacrosse:
and it's not important who won.
But don't ask for my choice of games using a ball:
it's a toss-up, if you'll pardon my pun.

Metaphorically Speaking

Like breath condensing on glass,
or emitting fog in frost,
or inhaling strength from air;
like unsuspecting mastodons
grazing midst the foliage and grasses,
glistening like dewy jewels,
destiny pushes and rides its driven role
to fulfillment.

Fortune is like a mysterious, opaque cloak
blanketing the serenity of the habitual;
concealing, like some murky fog,
all of its intent and possibility.

Like the swoop of an avian avenger's claws,
the shock of reality reveals
the perishing of innocence.
The revelation, unhappily, like a trampled ant
or ensnared, be-webbed fly,
is belatedly and absurdly terminal.

Our daily lives tremble like delicate petals
engulfed in storm's attack, courageously
holding firm to a solid entrenched anchor,
like a helpless vessel in tormenting,
overwhelming surges.

When diminished winds enter placid, apologetic remorse,
with receding rivulets acting the role of innocent,
the final tableau of clown and demon,
balloon and dagger, takes its exiting bow
and rehearses for its next flamboyant visitation,
not unlike those roving thespians
or wandering gypsy bands.

The assessor's life-damage review seldom overtakes
the reality of loss's cost.
Lucky survivors' resolve and sinews are hardened,
skin thickened, scars concealed, clocks re-wound;
and discovering the strongest emotional adhesive,
permitting the restoration
of surrounding shards and fragments.

Awaiting the next testing.

Poet's Aid

The empty, hungry sheet of white
sits still with beggar's eye,
and pleads for life to banish naught,
with a barely audible cry.

Its partnering bringing mind to rest
in salute to creation's urge;
the challenged transfer of mist to earth,
crystallizes the creative surge.

Thus fulfilling its sibling role,
like a furnace receiving coal,
it rounds the cycle, transmuting thought,
reflecting the poet's goal.

Re-Wind

Too short awhile we stay on earth
from birth to sorrow's end.
Our deeds could stand a fresh review:
I hope there's time to mend.

Meaningful Sounds

The owl hoots and the lion roars;
the dog just barks "bow-wow."
The sheep says "ba-a-a" and the monkey howls.
I can't help but wonder how.

The kitten purrs, the hens cackle and cluck.
The horse just whinnies and neighs.
The rooster yells his "cock-a-doodle" song;
the donkey "hee-haws" and brays.

The cat says "meow" but the cow says "moo;"
the tiger stands and growls.
The frog sits on a rock and croaks;
the big gray wolf just howls.

The turkey struts and says "gobble-gobble"
and the tiny mouse will squeal;
The elephants trumpet, the eagles scream.
The wail of the loon has appeal.

The snorts, the buzz, the monkey's chatter;
the cacophony of mating sounds.
The grunt of pigs, the screech of crows,
the haunting of baying hounds.

The goose will honk, the moose will bellow;
the hiss of the frightened snake.
I'm amused and intrigued at the medley of sounds
that birds and animals make.

We humans talk and shout and laugh,
and also sigh, sing and cry.
But we're just another animal's sound
in Nature's objective eye.

Last Grad Standing

What, a strange feeling it would be
to attend one's college class re-union,
open the door, and discover
that you are the only one in the room:
the only remaining survivor
of your graduating class.

I've spoken to such a person,
one hundred years old.

BLUEPRINT

What guides and points the way
to life's pathways?
What mysterious gravity and pull
give drive, purpose and skill
in fulfilling one interest
over another?
What brain circuitry activates
towards quiet and serenity?

What drives the pursuit and participation
in this, over that?
What directs one to art, sport, teaching,
writing, music, science,
mathematics, exploration, invention,
entertainment, soldiering or politics?

Wheel Of Fortune

The feathered chief looks down and smiles
at Fortune's ironic twist:
revenge in casino form,
to help forget our merciless fist.

The tears that fell upon the plains,
those tents with apex-ed poles;
the ancient customs and tribal ways,
sundered by expanding goals.

But Fate laughs loud and makes amends
by having the victors pay;
a slight redress, we all agree,
for history's other day.

Now, wheel with ball goes round and round,
the blackjack tables full;
the dice roll noisily on the green,
and slots add to the thrill.

It'll take awhile to make them forget,
if ever that can be done…
but there is some jest in tables turned:
our lost bucks to casino's gun!

Social Animal

Have you ever noticed and observed
that some people need to talk
of themselves alone in endless stream:
your blackboard to their chalk.

They only seek a set of ears
to hear of themselves alone;
uninterested in another's life,
and not hearing their repressed moan.

It's a boring display and all one-way,
an ego-induced domination.
The poor captured listener deserves some pity,
a reluctant party to such "conversation."

Transported

What anticipated pleasure, mystery, curiosity
await youthful expectation
upon hearing, or seeing,
the magical words:
"Once upon a time..."

More Than Just Friends

We're on the same wavelength, you and me,
we usually see eye to eye.
When you itch, I scratch; you inhale dust, I sneeze.
We both like bargains to buy.

We're stems arising from a single root.
Our thoughts flow one from another!
If you're hungry, I eat, if thirsty, I drink,
as if cast from a single mother.

But differences show, which shouldn't surprise,
such as mattresses hard or soft.
I can't stand cold and prefer warmth,
while you thrive in the snow and the frost.

I've known you as long as I know me.
We've been through a lot on this road:
our homes and our jobs and through health and the sick,
we each have partnered the load.

Yes, traveled we have, through bad and the good,
experiencing fashion and trend.
I'm so thankful to you and our nesting and love…
You're still my very best friend!

Withdrawal

When this world's crowded din intrudes
and rife ignorance overwhelms,
what may offer respite's calm
is a hermit's peace.

Passing Encounter

I love to see the head of a dog
sticking out, taking in sights
through the rolled down window of a passing car,
claiming its canine rights.

He tries to make contact as we ride side by side
from his chauffeured, coddled nook.
The wind roughs up his hair, his eyes glistening so
with a "I-want-to-get-to-know-you" look.
Sometimes, I notice an "I'm somebody!" stare,
on an adventure so memorable and fine.
A brief friendship can flourish as our moving eyes lock
between his open window and mine.

Merry You Know What

With a "HO! and a "HO!" and a one more "HO!"
the fat old man will sing
a merry old tune that warms the heart
on this day where he's the king.

His bag is heavy and his back is bad,
he'd rather be in bed.
But duty calls and young ones wait
(so much for thoughts of Club Med!).

With a shrug of shoulder, a sigh and deep breath
and a dutiful "Giddyap!" shout
the laden sleigh with a shuddering lunge
would lighten before the night was out.

But we must not forget his wife at home
who helps to get him dressed;
who combs his beard and sews the bells
(the big man knows he's blessed!).

She pays the cleaning bills on time
and feeds the grateful deer.
Santa may be the red-suited star
but she, too should get the cheers!

So, sing your songs, and drink your nog,
and sleepy ones wait up.
This holiday makes us all like kids.
We never want it to stop!

Judgments

We think it odd and "primitive"
when reading of earth's strange places.
We gawk and smile at garish stripes
and tattoos on body and faces.

Some lips are stretched and necks are ringed:
we think it peculiar and strange;
so "picturesque" and so unlike us
and such a cultural change.

They decorate skin and knot their hair,
and we are so amused;
or whitened face or bone-in-nose;
we hope their body's not abused!

We smile at their feathers, bells and grass skirts,
and carved-head masks made of wood.
Their communal dancing, clapping and song
is so different and not understood.

However, have we critically considered
our own peculiar ways?
We brag about our civilized heights
but what of another's gaze!

If others would see us in our living mode,
objectively viewed afar,
there'd be no wrong or right to say
but keep judgment's door ajar.

Our red painted lips, the rouged-on cheek,
hair waved and dyed so brash;
the powders, sprays, mousse and jells,
the mascara and curled eye lash.

The ornamental beads, earrings and bangles,
nails painted on hands and toes;
tattooing our own skin has become our own fad,
and don't forget our furs, ribbons and bows.

Our bodies are waxed, removing all hair,
we tan to avoid looking pale.
We pierce nostrils, tongue, ears and more
and attach rings to augment the tale!

Now, who is to say which culture is stranger?
Some others may not be for us.
But everyone lives in styles all their own.
Accept it…and why all the fuss?

Home Sweet Home

Our home is one in inter-locking harmony,
and delicate balance;
an intricate, living, finite
and pulsating creation,
not appreciative of the spoiling
and fouling of our only nest.

Prove It!

I showed a poem I wrote some years ago
to a room-mate whose opinions I sought.
I thought it was good and hoped he did, too,
but it was a lesson I had to be taught.

He read it through and then again,
then looked up at me and said:
"You're kidding, of course, you couldn't write this…
you copied it!" and my face turned red.

"Don't fool me again!" he seriously said.
"Show me the rough drafts you wrote!"
I was embarrassed to say I had thrown them away,
and the words just stuck in my throat!

For, I had tried to be tidy and threw away the notes,
thinking that the poem was enough.
But from that moment on, I resolved to store drafts;
for some experiences just make you tough.

So, drawers and boxes are filled with my work,
scribbled in pencil or pen.
Now you can ask me if my poems are mine
and I'll steer you to bedroom and den.

Floral Journey

From seeded birth to petal'd stem,
I basked in rays so warm,
inhaling life and nature's smile,
swaying in my flowery dorm.

How fast, it seemed, before I knew
my seedling's path to prime:
a flourished path to colored prize,
and scented kiss to time.

My parting from my neighbored home,
and roots that fed my life;
my bewildered and truncated peace
succumbed to a gardener's knife.

When next I knew, I shared a space
with other flowered kin,
exchanging tales and seeking homes,
and hoping hearts to win.

The moment came when I was picked
together with vase mates,
and bundled close with ribboned touch,
ending impatient waits.

For next we knew, this fragrant gift
was held and loved so much;
and we all agreed this purposed end,
was our Fate's final touch!

Not A Bad Fad

Peter was a serious kid,
normal in every respect.
He had one unusual trait:
he spoke like you'd never expect.

Whenever he talked his words had to rhyme,
for Peter was a very good poet.
His teachers and parents all marveled in awe.
He was talented and couldn't help but show it.

Whenever he spoke, his friends thought it was a joke,
for he spoke in a way never heard.
He'd say "Let us play. It's such a fine day!"
The street kids thought it absurd.

Now who would believe, unless you're naive,
that he'd be a sought after friend.
But, strange as it seems, his rhyming was catchy,
for he created a fad and a trend.

The news got around that a fad had been found,
rhymed verse is the way every kid spoke.
Once ostracized Peter, the butt of such laughter,
said:"Everything's now okee-doke!"

Hm-m-m, Now Let Me See...

Scratching one's head in puzzlement
at some unresolved quiz or thought,
has always strangely bothered me
as a way for answers sought.

That phrase is used so many times
in stories I have read,
and each and every time I ask
what's wrong with that person's head?

Could it be a case of rash
that causes such need to scratch;
or could it be some tiny bugs
that help solutions hatch.

This phrase is used so frequently
by writers over time,
suggesting quizzical pondering
in helping to solve a crime.

I've yet to see in my daily life
this act that helps shed light:
a scratching of head when perplexed,
which doesn't seem quite right.

Enigma

Of all the possible and puzzling mysteries
to dwell upon,
as we review our life's course and fortunes,
the single most intriguing is:
"What if...?"

Image And Truth

Addressing a world conclave, or Congress, at least,
with microphone open to the world;
or receiving gold medals for astonishing feats,
or bringing peace to the embroiled;
no matter the target, no matter the goal,
the hours and sweat must be dues.
It's easy to long for success and applause,
but day-dreaming's no option to choose.

It's not realistic to expect crops to thrive
without effort or water or seed.
There's cost to be paid for accomplishing ends:
dreams alone cannot fill the need.

Such flowery passionate cheers of acclaim
can surround one in vanity cloak,
for they've already achieved what they've wanted to do
so, why bother with effort's yoke!

"Nothing for nothing!" has often been said
to those hopeful for boastful acclaim,
who rely on fanciful musing instead
as the easiest path to fame.

Awesome

My voice was fantastic! A triumph of tone with such dazzling vocal power; spectacular, thrilling...until I hurt myself taking bows in the shower.

Hello Again

When spring shows up with its slow arm-stretching
and picks up after last year's goodbyes,
the greeting hellos and breaths of relief
fill pockets of shivers and sighs.

The gloves, the scarves, boots and "Long Johns"
are replaced now with adornments of spring.
The scarves and boots and pipes that were frozen,
are nothing to which I resentfully cling.

The shovels and muffed hats, sweaters and wools,
the icicles and logs that won't burn:
the sleds and the skis I joyfully trade
to see song birds and petals and fern.

Poetic Expression

What would be written without clouds or the sun
or rain or season's succession;
or infants with sounds of needing and wants,
contributing to a poet's expression.

The flowers and birds, the feeling of awe,
at mountains overwhelming our sight:
urge pen to record and feelings stripped bare
at nature's delicacy and might.

We record tastes of food and love's twinkling eyes,
excited as a child in a toy store;
reveling at the choices afforded by life
of subjects, feelings and more.

Our ink may run dry for each moment is full:
and sharing is what we must do.
The impulse of poetry is revealing ourselves
describing some bubble of life's brew.

Some may see deeply and some may cavort,
some of us tell of our day;
hoping to entrance within subtlety's web,
hoping to weave gold out of hay.

Some poems are diaries of events, then and now,
with details minor or sweeping:
metaphorically rich or playful with image,
a few drops or generously heaping.

Alternatives

Nature has thoughtfully provided us
with a natural balancing scale,
a tool,
for fairly weighing our options,
choices, views and decisions,
rationally pitting fact against fact,
best described as:
"On the one hand...but on the other hand..."

Share

When facing a sheet that's blank and dry
and that's begging for a drink
from your creative, poetic barrel of wit,
don't pull back from the brink.

Take a breath and start to write,
for you know there's much to tell.
There's an inner urge to share what's seen,
and inner thoughts, as well.

What adds some fun to making verse,
and challenges the task,
is adding rhyme and meter's pace.
What more can a poet ask?

There's so much memory in our pouch,
things left undone and done:
our sightings of the views so rare,
and personal races won.

Our friends come flickering across the screen,
our adventures bring a smile;
our travels, hopes and people met
(some filled with wile and guile!)

So, write or type or tell your tales
imagined, or what's real.
Our journey's unfulfilled until
you tell us how you feel.

About The Author

Nathan Polsky, author of this collection of poems, is a native New Yorker. He has been married for over sixty-four years to a woman with whom he attended their high school prom. They have two daughters.

He was an elementary school art teacher, cartoonist, illustrator, fabric designer and artist. His work appeared in various newspapers and periodicals. He won an award from the New York Art Directors Club for a work commissioned by CBS. He is still a working artist.

During World War II, he was a bombardier, flying over two dozen missions, earning a Purple Heart and two Bronze Stars.

Polsky has a BS and an MA degree from NYU. His professional career included being Director of several community arts organizations, Project Director at Macmillan and Houghton Mifflin publishers, and advertising manager with several paper companies.

He founded and was president of Scratch-Art Co., an arts and crafts company, inventing and manufacturing many original creative art products for schools and commercial markets before finally selling the company and retiring.

For the last several years, he has concentrated on writing poems, focusing on personal thoughts, observations, experiences, memories, etc. seeing the serious and humorous sides of life. His poetry is thought-provoking, silly, funny, and sometimes with themes that are perceptive and disturbing. These poems are the fruits of a long participatory life and should be shared.

Now also available in eBook and digital formats. Visit Amazon, or Barnes & Noble, or other on-line book sellers or contact the publisher for traditional print or alternative formats.

Meaningful Sounds
Copyright ©2013 by Nathan Polsky
All rights reserved.

Published By

Suncoast Digital Press, Inc.
8047 Royal Birkdale Circle
Lakewood Ranch, Florida, 34202

www.suncoastdigitalpress.com

www.ingramcontent.com/pod-product-compliance
Lightning Source LLC
Chambersburg PA
CBHW070642050426
42451CB00008B/270